A Note from
Mary Pope Osborne About the

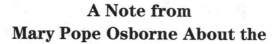

When I write Magic Tree House® adventures, I love including facts about the times and places Jack and Annie visit. But when readers finish these adventures, I want them to learn even more. So that's why we write a series of nonfiction books that are companions to the fiction titles in the Magic Tree House® series. We call these books Fact Trackers because we love to track the facts! Whether we're researching dinosaurs, pyramids, Pilgrims, sea monsters, or cobras, we're always amazed at how wondrous and surprising the real world is. We want you to experience the same wonder we do—so get out your pencils and notebooks and hit the trail with us. You can be a Magic Tree House® Fact Tracker, too!

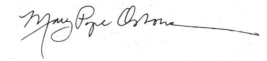

Here's what kids, parents, and teachers have to say about the Magic Tree House® Fact Trackers:

"They are so good. I can't wait for the next one. All I can say for now is prepare to be amazed!" —Alexander N.

"I have read every Magic Tree House book there is. The [Fact Trackers] are a thrilling way to get more information about the special events in the story." —John R.

"These are fascinating nonfiction books that enhance the magical time-traveling adventures of Jack and Annie. I love these books, especially *American Revolution.* I was learning so much, and I didn't even know it!" —Tori Beth S.

"[They] are an excellent 'behind-the-scenes' look at what the [Magic Tree House fiction] has started in your imagination! You can't buy one without the other; they are such a complement to one another." —Erika N., mom

"Magic Tree House [Fact Trackers] took my children on a journey from Frog Creek, Pennsylvania, to so many significant historical events! The detailed manuals are a remarkable addition to the classic fiction Magic Tree House books we adore!" —Jenny S., mom

"[They] are very useful tools in my classroom, as they allow for students to be part of the planning process. Together, we find facts in the [Fact Trackers] to extend the learning introduced in the fictional companions. Researching and planning classroom activities, such as our class Olympics based on facts found in *Ancient Greece and the Olympics,* help create a genuine love for learning!" —Paula H., teacher

MAGIC TREE HOUSE® FACT TRACKER

Pilgrims

A NONFICTION COMPANION TO MAGIC TREE HOUSE #27:
Thanksgiving on Thursday

BY MARY POPE OSBORNE
AND NATALIE POPE BOYCE

ILLUSTRATED BY SAL MURDOCCA

A STEPPING STONE BOOK™
Random House 🏠 New York

The Magic Tree House Fact Tracker series was formerly known as
the Magic Tree House Research Guide series.

Visit us on the Web!
MagicTreeHouse.com
randomhousekids.com

Educators and librarians, for a variety of teaching tools, visit us at
RHTeachersLibrarians.com

Library of Congress Cataloging-in-Publication Data
Osborne, Mary Pope.
Pilgrims / by Mary Pope Osborne and Natalie Pope Boyce ; illustrated by Sal Murdocca.
p. cm. — (Magic tree house fact tracker)
Includes index.
Reprint of 2005 ed. Series has new name.
"A nonfiction companion to Magic Tree House #27: Thanksgiving on Thursday."
"A Stepping Stone book."
ISBN 978-0-375-83219-2 (trade) — ISBN 978-0-375-93219-9 (lib. bdg.) —
ISBN 978-0-307-97531-7 (ebook)
1. Pilgrims (New Plymouth Colony)—Juvenile literature. 2. Massachusetts—
History—New Plymouth, 1620–1691—Juvenile literature. I. Boyce, Natalie Pope.
II. Murdocca, Sal, ill. III. Osborne, Mary Pope. Thanksgiving on Thursday.
IV. Title. F68.O83 2011   974.4'02—dc22   2011007035

Printed in the United States of America
28 27 26 25 24 23 22 21 20 19 18

This book has been officially leveled by using the F&P Text Level Gradient™
Leveling System.

In memory of our father,
William Perkins Pope

Historical Consultant:
CAROLYN TRAVERS, Research Manager, Plimoth Plantation, Plymouth, Massachusetts

Education Consultant:
HEIDI JOHNSON, Earth Science and Paleontology, Lowell Junior High School, Bisbee, Arizona

Very special thanks to Paul Coughlin for his great photographs; and to the terrific team at Random House: Joanne Yates, Mallory Loehr, Angela Roberts, and our editor, Diane Landolf, who helped every step of the way.

PILGRIMS

Contents

Dear Readers,

   <u>Thanksgiving on Thursday</u> made us curious about the Pilgrims. Who were these people? Why did they risk everything to travel to a new land? We had so many questions that we decided to do some fact-tracking.

   We began our search at the library. Sometimes it's hard to find enough books on a topic, but not on the Pilgrims! The shelves were packed with good information. We went home from the library loaded down with books. Then we went to our computers. Again we found more facts than we could ever use. It's important to use the best sites when you track

facts on the Internet. It helps to ask your teacher if you're not sure which websites to use.

The Pilgrims came alive for us through our research. We could read what people who were actually at the first Thanksgiving wrote about it. So sharpen your pencils, get your notebooks, and come be fact trackers like us!

Jack

Annie

1

Pilgrims Set Sail

In September 1620, a ship sailed from Plymouth, England. It was called the *Mayflower*. The passengers were headed for America, which Europeans often called "the New World." They would travel thousands of miles across the Atlantic. The voyage was long and dangerous. But this was a special trip. These people were leaving England to begin new lives.

Why would anyone undertake this hard journey? The people on board had different reasons. Some left because they had separated from the Church of England. They are called the *Separatists* (SEH-puh-ruh-tists). The Separatists wanted to worship their own way.

The king was head of the English church. He would not give them this freedom. He even put some of them in jail. There were about 37 Separatists among the passengers.

There were other people on board as well. They were not Separatists. They hoped to make a better living in the New World. There was not enough work in England. Among the group were farmers, woodworkers, shopkeepers, blacksmiths, weavers, and servants.

Altogether, there were 102 passengers on board . . . about 50 men, 20 women, and 32 children. Today we call all of these people *Pilgrims*.

The Long Voyage

There were supposed to be two ships going to America, the *Mayflower* and the *Speedwell*. But the *Speedwell* leaked badly. It couldn't make the trip. All but 20 of its passengers jammed onto the *Mayflower*. Living on board was not pleasant!

For the next two months, the journey was very scary. High winds and waves tossed the ship about like a toy.

The *Mayflower* was actually a cargo ship. It did not usually carry passengers. There were too many people on board.

The _Mayflower_ was only about 106 feet long and 25 feet wide.

They huddled together in a dark, cramped area under the main deck.

16

There was not enough fresh water. The ship did not have any bathrooms. They used vessels called *chamber pots* instead.

Chamber pots were emptied into the ocean.

The air quickly became foul and smelly. If clothes got wet, they stayed wet. Soon the passengers began to get sick. One of them died. The anxious Pilgrims often gathered to pray and sing. In November, their trip came to an end. After two long months, they finally sighted land.

A baby was born during the trip. He was named Oceanus Hopkins!

The Mayflower Compact

Tempers had grown short during the trip. People began to argue. So just before the ship anchored, the Pilgrims decided to write down some rules. They hoped this would stop the arguments.

17

Their agreement has come to be known as the *Mayflower Compact*. It was the first time in America that people wrote down ideas about governing themselves.

A compact is an agreement.

Like many paintings, this one of the compact signing shows the Pilgrims in clothing from the wrong period.

The compact was very short. But it said very important things. It said the people were united in their belief in God. They pledged their loyalty to the king and England. They promised to pass fair and just laws.

Forty-one men signed the compact. The Pilgrims voted for John Carver as their new governor.

Unfair! Women could not sign the compact. They did not have the same rights as the men.

The *Mayflower* had reached the coast of what is now Massachusetts. It anchored off of Cape Cod. The people felt their prayers had been answered. They fell to their knees and gave thanks. They were overjoyed to have found dry land.

The Pilgrims could not know that even worse times still lay ahead. All the rules in the world could not help them survive.

The <u>Mayflower</u>

There were 30 sailors on board.

Captain's cabin

Pilgrims slept in hammocks or on the floor.

The <u>Mayflower</u> was a little longer than a tennis court. It traveled about 2 miles an hour and covered 3,000 miles.

Sailors turned the sails with ropes to catch the wind.

Galley, or kitchen

Cargo and supplies

2

The New World

The ship was now anchored off the coast of Cape Cod. The Pilgrims climbed in a long-boat and rowed to shore. They found a country full of woods. Although there were many native villages in the area, the Pilgrims did not see them. All they could see was wilderness.

Once on shore, the women pulled out their washing tubs. They washed clothes all day. The children were free to run and play.

And the men began making plans to explore. They needed to find fresh water. And they were eager to find a good place to live and plant crops.

Exploring Cape Cod

A soldier named Myles Standish was chosen to lead some of the explorers. As they were scouting around, they came across a group of Native People. The natives ran back into the woods.

Native People had lived on Cape Cod for thousands of years.

Later, the explorers found a basket. It was full of corn kernels. The corn had been saved by a native family. Myles and his men thought it would be good for planting. They took it and planned to replace it or pay for it later.

Exploration continued on the cape. The Pilgrims could not agree on a good

They named this place Corn Hill.

spot to settle. The weather got colder. Winter was setting in. People began to get sick. They were running out of food.

The Pilgrims stole more from the Native People. The natives were wary and often ran away when they arrived. Some Pilgrims felt bad about the stealing. Later, they tried to replace some things they had taken.

Four people had died by the time the Pilgrims reached Plymouth.

27

The Pilgrims decided that Cape Cod was not a good spot. The water around the cape was too shallow. Ships could not anchor close enough to land to unload supplies. The Pilgrims worried there were too many Native People. They also worried about having enough fresh water. They decided to look elsewhere.

Master Jones's Map

The *Mayflower*'s master, Christopher Jones, had maps of the coastline. They were made by a man named John Smith. He was the leader of a group who had settled in Jamestown, Virginia.

Later, John Smith had sailed around the coasts of Maine and Massachusetts. In 1614, he made maps of what he had seen.

Prince Charles of England looked at the maps. He named this part of America "New England."

This is John Smith's map of New England.

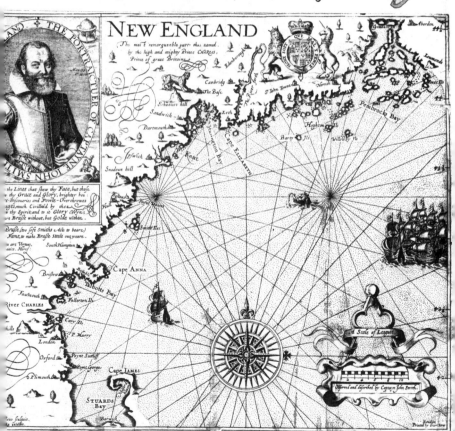

Plymouth

In December, several men set out in a small boat called a "shallop." They were looking for a place one of them had seen before. A storm whipped up. Winds and tides carried the boat toward shore. The men found themselves in a good harbor. This was the spot they were searching for.

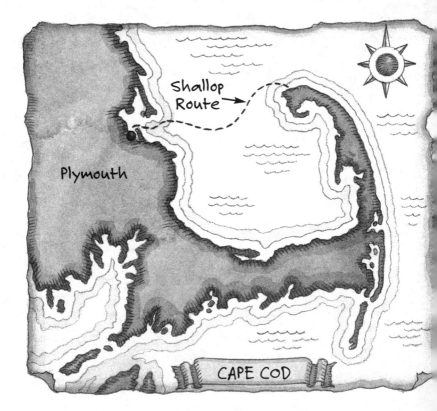

The Pilgrims land at Plymouth.

To their delight, they found a fresh-water river. They found cleared fields and they saw no Native People. It seemed the perfect place! They hurried back to the *Mayflower.* Captain Jones checked the map. Sure enough, it showed the harbor. The king had named it Plymouth (PLIH-muth) after a town in England. The *Mayflower* arrived there three days later.

Plymouth was the site of an abandoned native village.

Plymouth Rock

There is a *legend* that the Pilgrims first stepped onto a certain rock when they landed. The rock actually exists. It is called "Plymouth Rock." Even today many people believe the legend of Plymouth Rock. But experts are not positive that the story is true.

In 1774, a group of men tried to move the rock to a special place in the town of Plymouth. The rock cracked in two. Sixty oxen dragged the top half to the liberty pole in the town square.

In 1834, they moved it again . . . this time to a museum in Plymouth called Pilgrim Hall. Later, the rock was moved several more times. Today it sits near the water, the top half cemented to the bottom.

Over the years, people have chipped away at Plymouth Rock. Everyone wanted to take a piece for themselves. Now it is one-third of what it used to be! An iron fence protects the poor rock. Over 800,000 people visit it every year.

3

The Wampanoag

When Captain John Smith first explored the coast of New England, he saw fields and houses. These belonged to Native People. Today we know them as the Wampanoag (wahm-puh-NO-ag) Nation. This means "People of the First Light" or "People of the East." They were hunters, gatherers, farmers, and fishermen.

The Wampanoag had lived in New

England for over 12,000 years. In the early part of the 1600s, there were about 50,000 Wampanoag living in 69 villages. Groups were known by the place where they lived. For example, if they lived in Patuxet (puh-TUX-it), they were called the Patuxet.

Many villages were completely deserted.

When the Pilgrims arrived, about half of the Wampanoag had died of disease.

Wampanoag Government

Each Wampanoag group had its own leader called a *sachem* (SAY-chum). The sachem was not like a king. He led because of his ability and his family. A sachem worked like everyone else. He was there to listen to advice and make decisions.

Women could become sachems if the old sachem had no son.

The Wampanoag did not have written

rules. Instead, they had *traditions* (truh-DIH-shunz) they'd followed for many years.

Traditions are ways of doing the same things from generation to generation.

All the different groups met. They discussed their problems. Then they voted on a solution.

Discussions could concern their hunting grounds. Each family had its own land for hunting. These lands passed from fathers to sons. Protecting their hunting grounds was very important to them.

Wampanoag Villages

The Wampanoag built longhouses for meetings. Families lived in round houses made of reed mats or bark. They were called *wetus* (WEE-tooz). Wetus had holes in their roofs. Smoke from cooking fires escaped through the opening.

Building a wetu.

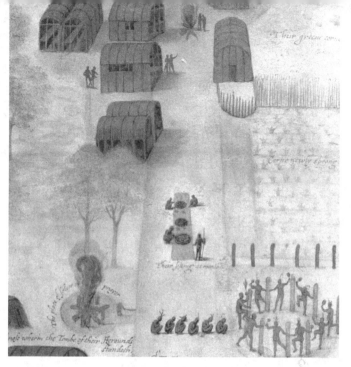

This watercolor of a native village was
painted in the 16th century.

Villages usually had fields around them.
The Wampanoag grew pumpkins, corn,
squash, melons, sunflowers, and beans.
After the harvest, they stored the best
seeds for the next year's crops.

The Wampanoag also grew tobacco. They smoked socially and during ceremonies.

Summer was the growing season. Families moved close to the shore. They planted crops in the nearby fields. They also fished and dug clams.

In the fall, everyone moved inland. This was the time to hunt deer and bear. They fished by cutting holes through the ice on ponds and lakes.

Clothing

The Wampanoag wore clothes made of animal skins, usually deerskin. They often wore bone or shell necklaces. Feathers were used to make headpieces.

Feathers, especially turkey feathers, were sewn into the clothes.

In cold weather, they wore deerskin leggings to keep out the chill. They made warm fur cloaks from beavers and other animals. In warm weather, they went

40

barefoot or wore light deerskin shoes called "moccasins" (MOCK-uh-sinz). Winter moccasins were covered with fur.

Bone necklace

Fur cloak

Deerskin skirt

Breech-clouts

Noohkik pouch

Deerskin leggings

Deerskin moccasin

Celebrations

The Wampanoag people gave thanks every day. But every year they had a special celebration of thanksgiving called "Nickommo." It was held in December. During this time, the Wampanoag gave away goods to those in need. They danced, ate, played games,

and sang a lot. (One Pilgrim wrote that when he passed a village at night, he could hear them singing themselves to sleep.)

There are still Wampanoag people in New England today. And many celebrate Nickommo just as their people did so long ago.

Wampanoag Children

Wampanoag children lived active lives. Boys practiced shooting with small bows and arrows. When they were old enough, they hunted and fished with their fathers.

Girls practiced making pottery, sewing, and weaving. They also helped their mothers in the gardens and around home.

Like all children, they liked to have fun. During the day, they played games. Swimming was a favorite summer activity. Since they often traveled in canoes, they learned to swim at an early age.

In the winter, their elders told stories full of tribal history and important lessons. One of their favorites was about the sachem Moshup, a giant so large he often ate whales!

Cruel Treatment

For a hundred years before the Pilgrims arrived, explorers, traders, and fishermen had been visiting New England. Sometimes they went about their business in peace with the Native People. But often there was trouble between the two groups.

Sometimes the strangers treated the Native People badly. They shot at them without reason. They stole their corn and furs. Sometimes they even captured them and sold them into slavery.

Too often, Native People died from diseases the newcomers brought. These diseases were different from any they

This woodcut shows a Wampanoag village overcome by disease.

had ever caught before. Their bodies had no way to fight the new infections. Whole villages were wiped out.

Later, more settlers arrived. They forced the Native People from their lands. Farms and towns grew up where native villages had once stood.

4

Hard Times

The Pilgrims set about building a village. Winter had arrived. The weather became bitterly cold. Rain, sleet, and snow pelted down as they worked. First they built a storehouse. At night, the builders slept there. The others slept on the *Mayflower*.

Now many Pilgrims became ill. One terrible disease they reported was *scurvy* (SCUR-vee). Scurvy is caused by lack of vitamin C from fresh fruits. A disease that

Scurvy makes your gums turn purple and bleed! Then your teeth fall out.

51

probably killed many was *pneumonia* (nuh-MOAN-yuh). Pneumonia is a serious lung infection.

January and February were the worst months. At one point, only six Pilgrims were well enough to work and care for the others. Governor John Carver died in the late spring. William Bradford was elected the new governor.

Bradford was governor for 33 years.

Bradford wrote a history of life in Plymouth. He said that sometimes two or three people died a day. At the end of winter, over half of the Pilgrims were dead. Almost every family lost a loved one. Only one family was spared from tragedy.

Four entire families died.

In spite of sickness and sorrow, the Pilgrims continued working. They laid out lots for houses along a short street. Then they began to build the houses.

At first, not everyone had their own house. Smaller families had to live together. Men who came alone lived with other families. Everyone was crowded. But it was more comfortable than the *Mayflower*.

After a year, there were only seven houses.

Samoset

One day, the Pilgrims had an unexpected visitor. A Native American strode alone into the village. He was a tall man who carried himself with dignity. Long black hair hung down his back. Imagine the Pilgrims' surprise when he greeted them in English!

The man's name was Samoset. He was

Samoset held up his hand and said, "Welcome, Englishmen!"

Samoset arrives at Plymouth.

from a native group in southern Maine. Samoset had learned some English from fishermen and other explorers.

The Patuxet died from diseases brought by explorers.

He explained that Plymouth had once been the village of Patuxet. The village had been wiped out by disease.

Samoset told the Pilgrims about other Native People living in the area. He visited three times. The third time he brought a Wampanoag man named Squanto.

Squanto

Squanto spoke English well. He had once been kidnapped by an English sea captain. The captain sold him into slavery in Spain. When he was finally freed, he made his way to England.

Squanto was from the Patuxet tribe.

Squanto lived and worked there for five years. Finally, he returned to New England. Sadly, all of his people had died of disease. Squanto was alone.

Squanto Helps the Pilgrims

Squanto could see the Pilgrims were in trouble. He decided to give them lessons on how to survive. First he taught them to plant corn. He told them to bury fish with their corn seeds. The fish rotted and acted as fertilizer.

They planted the corn stolen from the Native People on Cape Cod.

The Pilgrims had brought many seeds with them from England. But they were hard to plant with no plows. With Squanto's help, they were able to plant about 20 acres of corn and six acres of peas and barley.

Squanto led the Pilgrims into the fields and woods. Some people think that they searched for wild plants that were *edible* (ED-uh-bul). Then he showed them how the Native People fished and hunted in the area.

The Pilgrims' diet began to improve!

Squanto Helps Make Peace

Finally, Squanto helped the Pilgrims and the Wampanoag make an alliance. Chief Massasoit (MASS-uh-soyt) was a powerful Wampanoag leader. He and the Pilgrims met together. Squanto spoke both Massasoit's and the Pilgrims' languages. He helped them understand each other.

Massasoit signed a treaty of protection with the Pilgrims.

They all promised to return anything they had stolen from one another. They also vowed to defend each other from attacks by other enemies.

But Squanto was not always helpful.

Sometimes he caused trouble between the Wampanoag and the Pilgrims. He wanted to be an important native leader. At times he lied. Once he said the Pilgrims would send a terrible disease to the natives. This was not true. He was using his friendship with the Pilgrims to gain power.

No matter what his motives were, Squanto did help save the colony. For the rest of his life, he lived with the Pilgrims. In the end, they were so grateful to him, they called him "an instrument of God."

Turn the page to meet some of our favorite Pilgrims.

William Bradford, governor
(1590–1657)

William Bradford was a Separatist. He left England on the *Mayflower* with his wife. They had to leave their only child behind.

When the *Mayflower* was off Cape Cod, Mrs. Bradford fell overboard and drowned.

Later, William married again and had three more children.

As governor, William Bradford was a strong leader. During his term, he kept peace with the Wampanoag and other Native People. His wisdom and guidance helped the Pilgrims survive. A lot of what we know about the early Pilgrims comes from his *History of Plymouth Plantation.*

William Bradford

William Bradford's signature.

Captain Myles Standish
(1584–1656)

Myles Standish was a soldier. He came to Plymouth as a military adviser. Later, he became one of its best leaders.

Standish was a small, powerful man. Sometimes people mocked him because of his hot temper. But they also respected him and admired his bravery.

In the terrible winter of 1621, Myles's wife died. Myles was one of the few Pilgrims who did not get sick. William Bradford wrote that Myles bathed, fed, and nursed many sick people. Three years after that winter, Myles remarried. He and his wife had seven children.

Myles Standish's signature.

Priscilla Alden
(dates unknown)

Priscilla Mullins traveled on the *Mayflower* with her mother, father, brother, and a servant. Sadly, all of them died in the winter of 1621, and young Priscilla was left alone.

But not for long! A young man named John Alden took notice of her. They married and started a family. They went on to have 11 children.

Priscilla and John lived in Plymouth at first. After enduring the first hard years there, they moved to the village of Duxbury. No one knows the date of Priscilla's death.

John Alden
(1598–1687)

John Alden came to Plymouth when he was about 21. Governor Bradford called him "a young and hopeful man." For many years, he was a leader at Plymouth. People trusted and liked him.

Later, John and Priscilla moved to the village of Duxbury. But they still returned to Plymouth for church on Sundays. And they lived there in the winter.

Many years later, Henry Wadsworth Longfellow wrote a famous poem about John, Myles Standish, and Priscilla. It was called "The Courtship of Myles Standish." For years, schoolchildren read this poem. And long afterward, the names of these three people were famous because of the poem.

John Alden's signature.

John Alden died when he was very old. His and Priscilla's house still stands in Duxbury.

5

A Big Old Feast

The fall of 1621 was joyful. The Pilgrims had a great harvest! Everyone had worked hard. The storehouse was full of food for the winter. There was plenty of corn. There were salted meats and fish, and lots of vegetables.

In October, the Pilgrims felt grateful for their blessings. They were sure they would have food for the winter. They decided to

71

celebrate with a harvest festival. The 50 surviving Pilgrims met to praise God for their good fortune.

Guests at the Feast

Then it was time to plan the feast. It was to last for three days! Governor Bradford sent out four of his best hunters. After only a day of hunting, they returned with plenty of wild fowl.

That day they shot enough ducks and geese to last an entire week.

Meanwhile, Chief Massasoit arrived with 90 of his men. They shot five deer for the celebration. The whole village was bustling with activity.

Food for All

Only four married women survived the first winter. These women and the chil-

Women and children prepared food.

dren and servants set to work. They had a
lot to do! They began to cook. The women

Vegetables were called herbs; vegetable dishes were sallets.

boiled vegetables and stewed pumpkins. Since there was no sugar, they did not have pumpkin pie or cranberry sauce.

Have you ever tried eating unsweetened cranberries? Yuck!

Turkey may have been on the first Thanksgiving menu. In America, turkeys roamed wild in the woods. They didn't taste much like the turkeys we eat today.

They were more flavorful, but they could be tougher. The Pilgrims also ate deer, fish,

This illustration of the American wild turkey is by the famous bird artist John James Audubon.

stewed eels, ducks, and geese at the first Thanksgiving.

Setting the Tables

Workers set up tables throughout the village. They covered them with linen tablecloths. Then they set up benches, chairs, and even small barrels or baskets for seats.

Everyone brought out their eating utensils. These were knives and spoons only. Some of the Pilgrims carried knives with them all the time. They also had spoons. But no one used forks in those days.

The Pilgrims actually ate much of their food with their hands. This was really messy! So each guest used a *really* huge napkin. It was about three feet wide!

The women and girls set the table. They put out pewter and wooden dishes. Some of the wooden plates were square. They were called *trenchers*. Food was

The Pilgrims used items like these on their tables.

passed in serving bowls and on large platters. Everyone helped themselves.

Let's Celebrate!
The adults sat down to eat. It was the custom for children and servants to wait on the tables. They ran back and forth bringing food to the guests.

Children could not eat until everyone was served.

78

There was so much to eat, they feasted for several more days! Later, one of the Pilgrims wrote a letter home to England about the feast. "We had so much food," he said, "I wish you could have been here with us."

No pumpkin pie without sugar. It'll be dried berries as usual.

What's for dessert?

When the feasting was over, the celebration continued. The Pilgrims showed off their skills with their muskets. Perhaps Massasoit and his men sang and danced for the Pilgrims. There were probably races.

There may have been wrestling matches.

It was a time for enjoyment after all the hardships. It was a time for a great celebration.

America Celebrates Thanksgiving

Harvest festivals like the Pilgrims' were common in England. People feasted, danced, and probably drank a lot of beer.

In 1623, the Pilgrims held their first real Thanksgiving, "a time of praise and thanksgiving," with a daylong church service. Afterward, many towns in New England set aside a day for giving thanks in the fall or winter.

y the President of the United States of America.

A Proclamation.

The year that is drawing towards its close, has
n filled with the blessings of fruitful fields and
althful skies. To these bounties, which are so con=
ntly enjoyed that we are prone to forget the source
m which they come, others have been added, which

Lincoln declares the Thanksgiving holiday.

In 1863, Abraham Lincoln declared the last Thursday of November as a Thanksgiving holiday for everyone. But it was not yet an official yearly holiday. Finally, in 1941, Congress voted to make the fourth Thursday in November the annual day. And ever since, we all give thanks together at the same time every year.

6

Plymouth Grows

In November 1621, another ship arrived from England. It brought more people to Plymouth. Captain John Smith wrote that in 1624, about 180 people lived there.

Over the years, other ships followed. More houses went up. Plymouth began to look like a real village.

A Dutchman visited the town in 1627. His writings described the village. He noticed that the governor's house stood in the town's center. He said all the houses had neat gardens laid out in the back. There were larger buildings for storage and meetings.

But one building really impressed him. It was the fort. The Pilgrims built it for protection. They often met there as well. The fort was a large square building with a flat roof.

Six small cannons were on top of the building. They faced out in different directions.

A high wall also surrounded the town.

Houses

Houses in Plymouth looked a lot like houses in England. They are known as "wattle and daub" houses. A frame was put up and filled in with sticks. The sticks are called *wattle*. The wattle was covered

Early houses had a thatched
roof made of reeds.

with a mixture of wet clay, earth, and grasses. This is called *daub*.

Early on, the houses were small. Usually, there was only one main room downstairs. Sometimes there was a small loft upstairs. People usually stored things there.

The cloth or paper windows were oiled to bring in more light.

Most of the family life took place downstairs. There was a big fireplace for warmth and cooking. Windows let in some light. There were no glass panes until later. Instead, paper covered the openings. The houses were usually dim and smoky inside.

Preparing a meal took a lot of time.

Furniture

The Pilgrims brought some furniture with them. They did not have as much as we do today. To us, the houses look simple and bare.

People sat on benches or chairs. They had tables or used boards resting between barrels. Almost everyone slept on the floor on mattresses filled with straw. Many parents or the heads of a household had bedsteads.

If families did have chairs, they were for the adults only.

Some Pilgrims brought thick woolen rugs with them. They used them on the beds, not on the floor. During the freezing winters, the rugs came in handy!

Pilgrim families stored their clothes in wooden chests. They also hung them on hooks.

Inside a
Pilgrim House

Iron pots

Cradle

Oak chest

Dirt floors

Windows covered in oiled paper

Clothes hooks

Benches

Table made of board and barrels

Later, when the colonists built bigger houses, skilled furniture makers made more tables, chests, and chairs. They also built beds. The beds had springs made out of rope.

Mattresses lay on top of the ropes. If the ropes were not pulled tight, the bed sagged.

Beds had curtains to keep out the cold winter air.

Colonial maple and
ash chair

William Bradford's
silver cup

Myles Standish's
cooking pot

Clothing

William Bradford had a "turkey red" suit!

Many pictures show Pilgrims dressed in black and white and wearing buckled shoes. That's wrong! And if they owned any black clothes, they usually wore them only on Sundays. Most Pilgrims wore many different colors. They wore red, brown, green, blue, and violet. Clothes were either wool or linen.

Girls and boys wore gowns like this.

Little boys and girls both wore gowns. As boys grew older, they began to dress like the adult men.

Men wore long, loose shirts under their clothes.

Lace collar or ruff

Doublet

Cuffs

Breeches

Garters

Linen shirt

Woolen stockings

Women wore a long shirt called a "shift." They also wore corsets under their clothes and skirts called "petticoats."

Linen coif →

Waistcoat

Smock or shirt →

Skirt

Wool or linen apron

Leather shoes

Chores

There was a lot of work to do. There were no stores. There were no cars. Survival depended on hard work. The Pilgrims had no time for laziness. In fact, they passed a law against it!

Families worked together. People often had eight to ten children. The parents were very strict. The children worked as hard as the adults. They had to obey or else! They could not even speak unless spoken to.

Children were taught at home because the Pilgrims could not afford to set up a school.

There was corn to grind and washing to do. Girls and their mothers sewed. They cooked and cleaned. They watched the young children, tended gardens, and cared for livestock.

Boys and their fathers hunted and fished. They built houses, repaired tools, cleared land, and planted and tended crops. They also chopped down trees for lumber.

Every night, some of the men stood guard.

All day, people trudged back and forth to the springs with their water buckets. Morning and night, there were chores to do. The hard work was endless!

Jack's To-Do List
Help plant crops
Sharpen ax
Chop wood
Hunt and fish

Baths and Home Cures
If you hate to take a bath, you should have been a Pilgrim. They almost *never* took baths! They thought baths were not

good for them. Whew! No one knew being clean was healthy.

At times people got sick. There was no modern medicine. So women used plants from their gardens as medicine.

They boiled peppermint to make tea for upset stomachs. They cooked chicken soup and other home remedies.

Sometimes the cures worked. Sometimes they didn't. But all in all, visitors noticed the colonists seemed very healthy.

Church

Many of the Pilgrims had crossed the ocean so they could worship as they wished. They did not have a fancy church. They met in plain rooms, usually at the fort.

 This 19th-century engraving shows a Pilgrim church service.

No one worked or played on Sunday. Women cooked the day before. Sunday morning, the whole family was ready. At eight o'clock, they heard the sound of a drum. This was the signal to go to church. They all marched up the hill to the fort. Sometimes the minister talked for more than three hours!

It was a rule that men had to bring their guns to church in case of an attack.

Later, they went home to rest. In the afternoons, there was often more church!

Plymouth Today

Over time, the old village of Plymouth disappeared. It was slowly replaced by a modern town.

Years ago, people began to explore sites around Plymouth. They found broken pots, tools, and many other Pilgrim and Wampanoag *artifacts*. Artifacts are remains of things from the past. The artifacts gave researchers clues about daily life in Plymouth years ago.

They decided to build a village just like Plymouth in the 1600s. They built it near the town of Plymouth and called it Plimoth Plantation.

If you ever visit, you'll see daily life as it used to be. You can watch people living and dressing just as they did long ago. They even speak the way the Pilgrims did!

Plimoth is the old spelling of Plymouth.

7
The Future

After the terrible winter of 1621, the *Mayflower* sailed back to England. Master Jones offered to take anyone with him who wanted to return. Not one Pilgrim asked to return. Everyone was determined to stay . . . even after so much hardship.

There were still hard times ahead. The soil at Plymouth was poor. It was difficult to get enough food. The Pilgrims were sometimes hungry. But by 1623, they had learned how to make a living in the new land.

Crops improved. The Pilgrims began to fish and trade furs with Native People. And after 1623, they never starved again.

More people arrived. Many of them came in search of religious freedom. New towns began to spring up. By 1691, all these towns together made up the Massachusetts Bay Colony.

By 1643, there were ten towns around Plymouth.

Forty miles away, Boston became the most important city in Massachusetts. Plymouth stayed small. But today it remains one of the most famous places in the United States.

At Plymouth, the Pilgrims found the freedom they sought. They also found sadness, hunger, and death. But they never gave up. Their great adventure has become a symbol of the American spirit. Their story has grown into a legend. It's a story that all Americans can share and be proud of. And best of all, this legend is true.

Doing More Research

There's a lot more you can learn about the Pilgrims. The fun of research is seeing how many different sources you can explore.

Books

Most libraries and bookstores have lots of books about the Pilgrims and colonial life.

Here are some things to remember when you're using books for research:

1. You don't have to read the whole book. Check the table of contents and the index to find the topics you're interested in.

2. Write down the name of the book. When you take notes, make sure you write

down the name of the book in your note-book so you can find it again.

3. Never copy exactly from a book.
When you learn something new from a book, put it in your own words.

4. Make sure the book is <u>nonfiction</u>.
Some books tell make-believe stories about the Pilgrims. Make-believe stories are called *fiction*. They're fun to read, but not good for research.

Research books have facts and tell true stories. They are called *nonfiction*. A librarian or teacher can help you make sure the books you use for research are non-fiction.

Here are some good nonfiction books about the Pilgrims:

- *If You Sailed on the <u>Mayflower</u> in 1620* by Ann McGovern

- *<u>Mayflower</u> 1620: A New Look at a Pilgrim Voyage* by Plimoth Plantation, with Peter Arenstam, John Kemp, and Catherine O'Neill Grace

- *The Pilgrims of Plimoth* by Marcia Sewall

- *Pilgrims of Plymouth* by Susan E. Goodman

- *William Bradford: Plymouth's Faithful Pilgrim* by Gary D. Schmidt

Museums

Many museums have Pilgrim exhibits. They can help you learn more about the Pilgrims and the Wampanoag.

When you go to a museum:

1. Be sure to take your notebook!
Write down anything that catches your interest. Draw pictures, too!

2. Ask questions.
There are almost always people at museums who can help you find what you're looking for.

3. Check the calendar.
Many museums have special events and activities just for kids!

Here are some museums that have exhibits about the Pilgrims:

- Pilgrim Hall Museum (Plymouth, Massachusetts)

- Pilgrim Monument and Provincetown Museum (Massachusetts)

- Plimoth Plantation and *Mayflower II* (Plymouth, Massachusetts)

DVDs

There are some great nonfiction DVDs about the Pilgrims. As with books, make sure the DVDs you watch for research are nonfiction!

Check your library or video store for these and other nonfiction titles about the Pilgrims:

- *Desperate Crossing: The Untold Story of the Mayflower*
  from The History Channel

- *The Mayflower Pilgrims*
  from Janson Media

- *Plimoth Plantation,* Colonial Life for Children series
  from Schlessinger Media

The Internet

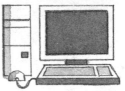

Many websites have lots of facts about the Pilgrims. Some also have games and activities that can help make learning about the Pilgrims even more fun.

Ask your teacher or your parents to help you find more websites like these:

- kids.nationalgeographic.com/kids /stories/history/first-thanksgiving

- mayflowerhistory.com/History /history.php

- pilgrimhall.org/museum.htm

- plimoth.org/kids

- scholastic.com/scholastic_thanksgiving

Good luck!

Index

118

Enough cool facts
to fill a tree house!

Jack and Annie have been all over the world in
their adventures in the magic tree house. And
they've learned lots of incredible facts along the
way. Now they want to share them with you! Get
ready for a collection of the weirdest, grossest,
funniest, most all-around amazing facts that Jack
and Annie have ever encountered. It's the ultimate
fact attack!

*Have you read the adventure that
matches up with this book?*

Don't miss

Magic Tree House® #27

THANKSGIVING ON THURSDAY

When the magic tree house whisks Jack and Annie
back to 1621 on the first Thanksgiving Day,
the Pilgrims ask them to help get things ready.
But whether it's cooking or clamming, Jack
and Annie don't know how to do *anything* the
Pilgrim way. Will they ruin the holiday forever?
Or will the feast go on?

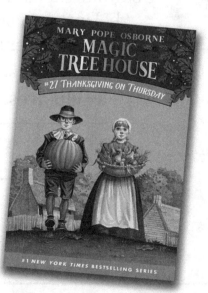

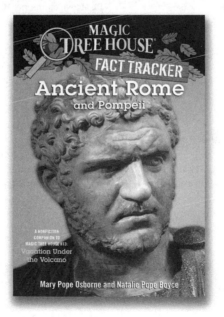

Magic Tree House®

Magic Tree House® Merlin Missions

Magic Tree House®
Super Edition

#1: WORLD AT WAR, 1944

Magic Tree House®
Fact Trackers

DINOSAURS

KNIGHTS AND CASTLES

MUMMIES AND PYRAMIDS

PIRATES

RAIN FORESTS

SPACE

TITANIC

TWISTERS AND OTHER TERRIBLE STORMS

DOLPHINS AND SHARKS

ANCIENT GREECE AND THE OLYMPICS

AMERICAN REVOLUTION

SABERTOOTHS AND THE ICE AGE

PILGRIMS

ANCIENT ROME AND POMPEII

TSUNAMIS AND OTHER NATURAL DISASTERS

POLAR BEARS AND THE ARCTIC

SEA MONSTERS

PENGUINS AND ANTARCTICA

LEONARDO DA VINCI

GHOSTS

LEPRECHAUNS AND IRISH FOLKLORE

RAGS AND RICHES: KIDS IN THE TIME OF
  CHARLES DICKENS

SNAKES AND OTHER REPTILES

DOG HEROES

ABRAHAM LINCOLN

PANDAS AND OTHER ENDANGERED SPECIES

HORSE HEROES

HEROES FOR ALL TIMES

SOCCER

NINJAS AND SAMURAI

CHINA: LAND OF THE EMPEROR'S GREAT
  WALL

SHARKS AND OTHER PREDATORS

VIKINGS

DOGSLEDDING AND EXTREME SPORTS

DRAGONS AND MYTHICAL CREATURES

WORLD WAR II

More Magic Tree House®

GAMES AND PUZZLES FROM THE TREE HOUSE

MAGIC TRICKS FROM THE TREE HOUSE

MY MAGIC TREE HOUSE JOURNAL

MAGIC TREE HOUSE SURVIVAL GUIDE

ANIMAL GAMES AND PUZZLES

MAGIC TREE HOUSE INCREDIBLE FACT BOOK

CALLING ALL ADVENTURERS!
Join the
MAGIC TREE HOUSE®
KIDS' ADVENTURE CLUB
Members receive:
• Exclusive packages delivered throughout the year
• Members-only swag
• A sneak peek at upcoming books
• Access to printables, games, giveaways, and more!
With a parent's help, visit MagicTreeHouse.com to learn more and to sign up!
© 2016 Mary Pope Osborne. Magic Tree House is a registered trademark of Mary Pope Osborne; used under license. Illustrations © 2016 by Sal Murdocca.